I See So

Text and Illustrations by Mike Artell

DOMINIE PRESS
Pearson Learning Group

ISBN 0-7685-0713-8

Printed in Singapore
3 4 5 6 7 8 07 06 05

Dominie Press
Pearson Learning Group

1-800-321-3106
www.pearsonlearning.com

This is a square.
Now here's what we'll do.
We'll look for squares
and read this book, too!

I see some squares.
Can you see them, too?
How many squares
can you find in this zoo?

I see some squares.

Can you see them, too?

Someone has squares on her dress.

Tell me who.

I see some squares.
Can you see them, too?
Show me the squares
all around this canoe.

I see some squares.
Can you see them, too?
Can you find the squares
in the picture he drew?

I see some squares.
Can you see them, too?
Where are the squares
near this funny cuckoo?

I see some squares.
Can·you see them, too?
It's a big square machine,
but what does it do?

I see some squares.
Can you see them, too?
Do you see the squares
on this funny old shoe?

I see some squares.
Can you see them, too?
Look for the squares
that are yellow and blue.

I see some squares.
Can you see them, too?
I see some squares
near the flowers she grew.

I see some squares.
Can you see them, too?
One square is easy,
but can you find two?

I see some squares.
Can you see them, too?
Where are the squares
near the cow that says, "Moo"?

I see some squares.
Can you see them, too?
Show me the squares
on this house that is new.

I see some squares.
Can you see them, too?
Do you see a bunch,
or only a few?